Bismillah hir rahman nir rahim
In the name of Allah,
The Most Gracious &
The Most Merciful

Hands Off Our Hijab

By Farhat Amin

www.smartmuslimah.com

Copyright Farhat Amin

Cover design: Farhat Amin

Editor: Ilham Ibrahim

All rights reserved. No portion of this book may be reproduced in any form without permission from the publisher. Except by reviewers who may quote brief passages in a review. For permissions contact hello@farhatamin.com

Hands Off Our Hijab

Putting liberal hypocrisy on trial

Farhat Amin

On the authority of Abu Saeed Al-Khudree (r.a.) who said: I heard the Messenger of Allah (sallallahu alaihi wasallam) say, "Whosoever of you sees an evil, let him change it with his hand; and if he is not able to do so, then [let him change it] with his tongue; and if he is not able to do so, then with his heart — and that is the weakest of faith." (Muslim)

CONTENTS

Introduction..7
1. A very French Inquisition 16
2. Historical unveiling of Muslim women by colonialists...............22
3. Time to play offence against the anti-hijab squad.....................35
4. Critiquing 'Headscarves & Hymens' by Mona Eltahawy............52
5. Material girls……... 63
6. Too afraid to wear hijab?...72
7. Good hijabis shatter stereotypes..84
8. India and the hijab ban by Hanan Khaja 93
9. About the author 111
10. References 112

Allah (swt) says in the Quran,

"They plot and plan, and Allah too plans; but the best of planners is Allah"

(Surah Al-Anfal, 8:30)

INTRODUCTION

In recent years, anti-Muslim sentiments have been on the rise. An increasing number of governments have capitalised on the global tide of Islamophobia to justify the state-sanctioned marginalisation of Muslims in their societies. Under the administration of French president Emmanuel Macron, Muslim women and girls under the age of 18 were prohibited from donning the hijab in public spaces. This degree of prejudice, however, is not exclusive to France. Earlier in 2021, the EU Court of Human Rights confirmed a law allowing companies to prohibit their employees from wearing hijabs at work. In Canada, a Quebec court upheld most of the law that prevents government workers from wearing hijabs. These totalitarian laws are comparable to the anti-Jewish laws introduced in Germany by the Nazis in 1933.

What was the response from the liberal progressive world? Shameful silence. At a time when Kamala Harris was being celebrated for her appointment as America's first woman of colour vice president and champion of democracy for women at the UN, her silence on France's overt Islamophobia was deafening. Even the usual commentators like Ayaan Hirsi Ali, Malala Yousafzai, and Angelina Jolie, who always have an opinion on the oppression of Muslim women, were all too silent. Why did they not speak truth to power? Surely they would organise the masses and demand an end to the infringement of individual autonomy as advocated by the very same liberal progressive states? At a time when intersectionality for women of colour came to be considered one of the most critical developments in women's rights, leaders of the movement and other prominent black figures chose to ignore the plight of Muslim women.

When Meghan Markle decided to reveal the details of the racism she and her unborn child had experienced in the UK, Muslims worldwide sympathised with the discrimination and prejudice they know all too well; they showed their solidarity with a woman of colour by posting on social media. They applauded Oprah for providing the platform to speak on the plague of racism. So why are both Meghan Markle and Oprah Winfrey, advocates for nearly every imaginable social issue, utterly silent on the racism of the French government? Why were they not outraged by the inequality and prejudice in Europe?

When election time came in the US, Muslim women worked tirelessly through every social media platform to encourage their communities to vote for Kamala Harris, A BAME liberal progressive woman who supposedly stood for women's rights. They tweeted and campaigned for who they believed would stand by them in their time of need. Now that she is in office, is she supporting her fellow BAME women in France? Why does female empowerment not extend to the Muslim women of Europe?

How many Muslim women looked up to Michelle Obama, bought her autobiography and applauded her outspokenness for justice and philanthropic work? Still, she is another famous woman of colour who has not explicitly condemned the rampant Islamophobia in France and elsewhere. It becomes imperative that we question our long-standing loyalties, support, votes and donations for such female figures who have proved that their calls for justice do not extend to Muslims. It's time we no longer blindly align ourselves with public figures who pay lip service to justice, anti-racism and women's rights only to ignore the institutional discrimination and inherent hatred towards Muslim communities in Europe right now.

In contrast, the most sincere people who spoke up for Muslim women were fellow Muslims motivated by a deep Islamic bond with their sisters. Rawdah Mohamed, a Somali-Norwegian model, started a campaign by posting a selfie on Instagram with "hands off my hijab" written on her hand. She said she wanted to challenge "deeply rooted stereotypes" against Muslim women. "I wanted my oppressors to see my face and the women who look like me," she said. "They don't get to hide in their luxurious parliament offices and regulate women's bodies without a fight."

Thousands of women internationally have used the hashtags #Handsoffmyhijab and #PasToucheAMonHijab to protest against France's xenophobic ban on the veil. Individually some non-muslims posted messages of support on social media. Still, unsurprisingly the lack of solidarity shown to Muslim women only reveals the selective morality of the liberal progressive world.

Prominent Muslim speakers, such as Omar Suleiman and Yasir Qadhi, were among many who strongly and eloquently condemned the fascist behaviour of the French government in their Friday sermons Muslim writers, YouTubers and podcasters-male and female-all used their platforms to support their sisters in France. Alhamdulillah, every voice raised to critique Islamophobia diminishes its impact. The global response of Muslims made me proud to be Muslim; it illustrated that we had internalised the following ahadith Narrated by Nouman ibn Bashir (r.a.) that the Messenger of Allah (saw) says: "The believers in their mutual kindness, compassion and sympathy are just like one body. When one of the limbs suffers, the whole body responds to it with wakefulness and fever" (Bukhari and Muslim).

And on the authority of Abu Saeed Al-Khudree (r.a.), who said: I heard the Messenger of Allah (saw) say, "Whosoever of you sees an evil, let him change it with his hand; and if he is not able to do so, then [let him change it] with his tongue; and if he is not able to do so, then with his heart — and that is the weakest of faith." (Muslim)

The hijab and niqab bans insidiously spreading across Europe have revealed a gaping wound at the heart of liberal society, an inherent intolerance that undergirds liberalism and its very foundations. Hypocritically, liberals pay lip service to justice, equality and women's rights and then conveniently turn a blind eye to the injustice meted out to Muslims. For all the talk of equality and human rights, liberalism suffers from what Bikhu Parekh calls profound narcissism. If you do not conform to the dominant consensus, you do not deserve equal recognition. This consensus is both intellectual and cultural. Those that refuse to embrace the hegemony of liberal values and who do not represent the cultural attitudes of the dominant group have all too often been marginalised and pushed to the fringes of societies.

So as believers, how should we respond to blatant attacks on our principles, dress code, and way of life? Why are non-Muslim politicians and governments vexed by the sight of a Muslim woman in a hijab? How can Muslims individually and collectively support our sisters who are being systematically targeted, repressed, and ridiculed? I intend to tackle these questions in this book. It is high time that we put liberal hypocrisy on trial. I sincerely want to help Muslimahs make sense of the complexity of these challenging times and take back control of the narrative. We must not forget, however, that reclaiming our narrative is not to be done on our own terms.

On the contrary, to break free from the hegemony of secular liberalism, we must restore our narrative on Allah's terms. Every law Allah gives us is a blessing. We are slaves of Allah and are bound to His command. The secular liberal world has overtly demonstrated that the supposed universality of human equality and individual autonomy does not extend to Muslim women, so why should we compromise our principles to please them?

I first began discussing the topic of hijab on my podcast Smart Muslima. I have explored issues such as "Why Has Liberal Switzerland Banned the Niqab?" and "The Politics of Hijab and

Hijab: Not My Body, Not My Choice." Witnessing the demoralising effects of the French hijab ban, I realised there was a need to articulate how hijabis feel about having their voice and identity erased by liberal fascists. Muslim women want to be seen and heard. We must be seen and heard not for the sake of tokenism or woke representation but for who we truly are and what we unapologetically stand for. When we raise our voices, we need to be grounded in the Prophetic tradition and sacred text with sincere conviction to articulate why we wear hijab and why we will never discard it. Additionally, I intend to address the lack of Islamic knowledge surrounding the obligation and method of wearing the hijab. We must anchor our actions and activism against discrimination and bigotry in the Quran and Sunnah.

The right book can make you feel less alone, less hopeless and closer to Allah. Inshallah, I pray that this book is the right book for you. It will help you make sense of the world so you can move forward confidently and comfortably in your hijab. It may seem like our enemies have the upper hand, but we have Allah on our side. The Creator of the universe, may He be exalted, says:
"Allah has promised those among you who believe, and do righteous good deeds, that He will certainly grant them succession to

(the present rulers) in the earth, as He granted it to those before them, and that He will grant them the authority to practise their religion, that which He has chosen for them (i.e. Islam). And He will surely give them in exchange a safe security after their fear (provided) they (believers) worship Me and do not associate anything (in worship) with Me. But whoever disbelieved after this they are the Fasiqoon (rebellious, disobedient to Allah). And perform As-Salat (Iqamat as-salat), and give Zakat and obey the Messenger (Muhammad saw) that you may receive mercy (from Allah)." (An-Noor 24:55, 56).

Let's remember each other in our duas.
Your Sister, Farhat Amin
www.smartmuslima.com

Narrated by Nouman ibn Bashir (r.a.) that the Messenger of Allah (sallallahu alaihi wasallam) says: "The believers in their mutual kindness, compassion and sympathy are just like one body. When one of the limbs suffers, the whole body responds to it with illness and fever" (Bukhari and Muslim).

Hands Off Our Hijab

A VERY FRENCH INQUISITION

When the French Interior minister Gérald Darmanin declared, "never at any given time, is Allah superior to the Republic." he echoed an emerging consensus in French political life – Islam has to be chastened and suppressed if Muslims are to be tolerated in the country.

For France's some six million Muslims, his intemperate remarks only served to underscore an intolerance to which the sizeable yet marginalised minority community have become accustomed. The political establishment left, and right perceives Muslims and their continued adherence to Islam as a danger to the republic and an affront to French secularism known as laïcité, a fundamentalist separation of religion from society that undergirds the republic.

As the state turns the screw on all Muslims by passing new draconian legislation, its experiment will serve as a blueprint for other European countries. At the centre of this offensive against the Muslim community is the so-called "anti-separatism" bill, given the

Orwellian sounding name, the law *"to reinforce the principles of the Republic and the fight against separatism"*.

The legislation has passed both houses of the legislature and has become law. The bill's provisions, crafted to incorporate all religions – lest it is challenged on discriminatory grounds – are directly aimed at coercing French Muslims into adopting the ideological dogma of the state. Homeschooling will be banned, and there will be an introduction of a child ID system for all over three years old, to track students in the educational system.

This serves to prevent parents who have chosen to educate their children at home, seeking to navigate the already harsh restrictions on hijab-wearing and muscular liberalism that restricts all forms of religious observance in educational settings. The bill increases the administrative powers of the state to shut down 'extremist' faith schools.

As Rayan Freschi, a French legal jurist, argues, this gives legal cover to the state's practice for many years, the use of schools inspectorates to close Muslim schools down on minor infractions. It is what has become known as a more comprehensive unstated policy of "systematic obstruction", employed by successive governments to undermine Muslim civil society institutions, such as mosques, schools and charities, by using existing provisions to make it impossible to remain open, often setting onerous fines or temporary closures to act as a disincentive against community initiatives.

The bill helps the state to more directly control what is being said in mosques, banning sermons that stray into politics or criticise, for example, French interventions in the Sahel and the Middle East. Religious leaders and organisations that receive public funds and tax exemptions would have to sign up to a 'charter of principles', explicitly declaring their allegiance to the French Republic.

Possibly the most egregious aspect of the bill bans the hijab in public for all under the age of 18. This measure, tabled by the French right, denies Muslim girls and women the right to wear the hijab anywhere in public. The wording of the clause talks of banning "signs or clothing" in public spaces that "ostensibly manifest a religious affiliation" or "that would signify the inferiority of women to men."

Emmanuel Macron's *En Marche* party opposed the amendment together with much of the left in the Senate, citing its unsubtle wording.Until now, the bill has steered clear of mentioning Islam directly, instead focussing on the façade that it represents an equal treatment of religion. Including the religious symbol clause removes any pretence and does what everyone knows the bill aims to do – further obstructing observant Muslims from practising their faith.

The bill also bans hijab-wearing mothers from accompanying their children on school trips. One left-leaning Senator, Mari-Noëlle Lienemann, explained her vote against the amendment by saying that she wanted to *"find legislation that outlaws the veil for minors,"* but that *"we cannot make a mistake in choosing which method to use"*. A former Socialist Party minister, J-P. Chevènement, who headed the government's *Fondation de l'islam*, declared, "The veil (hijab) is for many women an identity claim. This symbol means that marriage is only possible with a Muslim. This is a manifestation of separatism."

Like much of the political establishment in France, the progressive left subscribes to the aim of systematically obstructing Muslims but differ on the means. In 2004 it was the Socialist Party that banned the hijab in schools, and in 2010, President Sarkozy from the centre-right The Republicans banned the niqab using terrorism laws. Darmanin absurdly declared the amendment would harm "religious pluralism" in France. Yet, in the months before tabling the bill, he talked of his horror of halal-only food aisles in supermarkets. In an interview in *La Voix du Nord*, he floated the idea that Muslim women who refused medical treatment from male doctors could face heavy fines or even jail sentences. What is going on in France is nothing short of an inquisition. Even a charitable reading of the legislation would surmise it is aimed at all Muslims who observe Islam in their lives.

Its objective is to remove the usual organising capacities in Islamic communities that help foster a commitment to faith and at the same time forcibly convert young Muslims to embrace more stridently the commitments of the secular liberal republic.Recently, Darmanin had to reprimand two "overzealous" police officers when they asked a group of topless sunbathers to cover up on a beach, tweeting "it was wrong that the women were warned about their clothing" and "freedom is something precious", yet the same respect is not afforded to Muslim women, who face a daily barrage of racist slurs, discrimination and suspicion.

Some commentators have rightly pointed out that Macron's poor handling of the Covid crisis and the 'Yellow Vest' movement has harmed his prospect for re-election, citing the surge of Marine Le Pen's National Rally in the polls. Le Pen broke through to the second round in the last presidential election, a first for the French far-right. In a televised debate between Darmanin and Le Pen, the interior minister accused her of "going soft on Islam" because she had reservations about the separatism bill. In reality, the prospect of Le Pen winning may remain slight, but she is making ground in the polls. A second-round runoff may be closer this time than 2017, and Macron knows that to neutralise the non-committed right in the electorate, he has to outdo Le Pen and show a greater disdain towards Islam.

Yet to dismiss his position as merely posturing ahead of a general election would be naïve. The French state has embarked upon the systematic dismantling of the religion of Islam as practised by the majority of Muslims in the country.It is an acknowledgement that the 1905 law that explicitly removed religion from the public square has failed to diminish Muslim observance, resistant to attempts to secularise the faith.

Many in French society see Islam as a regressive religion, and, like attempts in colonial Algeria, nothing short of forcibly eradicating a religious culture can be entertained. Echoing its colonial past, there is a particular obsession with 'liberating' the Muslim woman, yet what is apparent is Muslim women, what they think and feel, is noticeably absent from the public discourse. This unsavoury direction of travel was underscored by an incendiary open letter in April written by a group of ex-generals who claimed "Islamism and the hordes of the *banlieue*" – the impoverished immigrant suburbs that surround French cities – was a recipe for "civil war".

In the absence of political and public pressure at home, Emmanuel Macron has a free hand to treat the Muslim community with the disdain that he has shown. Notwithstanding, recent protests and boycotts of French products after the cartoon controversy show that external pressure works if sustained. In the absence of meaningful international condemnation of France, a collective Muslim civil society effort to put pressure on the French government can temper the fundamentalism of the French state.- Macron was rattled late last year after the boycott started, having to appear on Al Jazeera to allay concerns.

He also took umbrage at an article in the Financial Times – now removed – written by a Muslim journalist about him. Instead, he penned his own op-ed, replete with erroneous slurs of Muslim girls as young as three forced to wear full-face veils, claims that have yet to be corroborated. Only coordinated civil society action can stop this template of suppression which may soon be borrowed soon by governments across Europe.

Alhamdulilah, Muslims are collectively accounting the French government for its anti-Muslim policies. In January 2021, a global partnership of civil society organisations submitted a detailed complaint[1] to the UN Human Rights Council (UNHRC) against France, requesting that it open a formal infringement procedure against the government for systematically entrenching Islamophobia and discrimination against Muslims.

"Muslims around the world united behind the cry to hold the French government accountable for continuing to support publications defaming the Prophet (saw). We hope they will unite again around this global-first, a truly collective effort, which expands the call for accountability and positive change."[2]

"France has seen shocking levels of state-sanctioned Islamophobia in recent months. This has precipitated the closure of mosques, Muslim schools, Muslim-led charities and civil society organisations. As a signatory to the UN, France cannot be allowed to infringe upon its international rights obligations so openly, and yet present itself as the land of 'liberté, égalité, fraternité'."[3]

HISTORICAL UN-VEILING OF MUSLIM WOMEN BY COLONIALISTS

The desire to unveil Muslim women is not a modern-day phenomenon. As European imperialism began to extend its hand into Muslim lands, colonial forces understood that occupying the hearts and minds of Muslim subjects was of equal concern. That is to say, in order to exert complete power and control, all that challenged the hegemony of European colonialism was to be excised from society, including Islam. Since the mid-19th Century, Muslims have been subject to a 'liberal inquisition'; we have been made to feel deficient and backwards when adhering to Islam. The colonial forces sought to undermine our values and way of life, leading to the widespread emergence of a type of inferiority complex.

Central to their schemes, the atomisation of the Muslim family was key. In particular, they targeted Muslim women. During the colonial period in many Muslim societies, Muslim women typically existed in spaces guarded against the peering eyes of strange men, thus entirely inaccessible to the colonial gaze. By forcefully reconstructing perceptions of gender, family, and social order in Muslim societies, the colonial forces were able to penetrate the physical and figurative spaces of Muslim women and impose an ideological worldview that was the antithesis of Islam. In other words, the European way of life was deemed universal, ethical, and cultured whilst Muslims were uncivilised people, living according to a moral code that harkened back to medieval days. When they came to our lands, they believed they were taming us. We were savages; they had to civilise us. Under the guise of "liberation", "humanitarianism" and false altruism, they claimed to "emancipate" us. We must then ask ourselves, from what exactly did they desire to emancipate us? Ultimately, it was to free us from Islam.

Let's look at the tactics used by occupying forces in Egypt, Algeria and Afghanistan. Lord Cromer, the British Consul General in Egypt from 1883 to 1907, was convinced of the inferiority of Islam

Muslim society and the "inferior mind of the Oriental". Islam's oppression of women and its insistence on veiling was the "fatal obstacle" to the Egyptian's "attainment of that elevation of thought and character which should accompany the introduction of Western civilisation". The Egyptians must be "persuaded or forced" to become "civilised" by discarding the veil. Hypocritically, Cromer founded and presided over the Men's League for Opposing Women's Suffrage in England. For the Egyptian woman, however, liberating her from the so-called Islamic patriarchy was essential.

Lord Cromer, like most colonial officers of his time, was not discrete in his disdain for Islam. Fundamentally, undermining Islam's influence in society, the dissolution of the Muslim family, and the unveiling of Muslim women were all tactics of control employed by the colonial forces to submit Islam to European dominance. Under the influence of Lord Cromer, Qasim Amin, a French-educated lawyer, wrote a book called The Liberation of Women (1899). He was also the leader of the Arab Liberal Party. The book was submissive in its praise of the west and harsh in its denunciation of Egyptian society. Amin asserted that Muslim societies had to abandon their backward customs and follow the western path to civilisation and success. What were these backward ways? Wearing the hijab and the Islamic social system. The European powers left a secular elite in the Muslim world that scoffed at Islamic practice and were besotted by the ostentation of European values. In 1830, French troops marched into Algiers, thus marking the beginning of over one hundred years of French colonial rule over Algeria. The period saw the violent suppression of Algerian resistance against French occupation. During this time, a nineteenth-century French official stated, "If we are to strike against Algerian society's capacity to resist, then we must, first of all, conquer their women," adding, "We have to go and find these women, under the veils they hide behind."[4]

The colonial desire to emancipate Muslim women could not have been executed without extensive state-funded propaganda. In fact, as French boots landed on Algerian soil military photographers were also enlisted to produce propaganda images in support of the colonial scheme back home. *In The Colonial Harem*, Malek Alloula highlights the extensive sexualised depictions of Algerian women by French colonists. Painstaking efforts were made to stage false representations of sexually-available Algerian women that, in truth, never existed. It is well-documented that these photographers hired poor and vulnerable women as unveiled models, lounging on cushions, often partially dressed or topless. "Upon arrival on Algerian soil, the French photographer faced a problem he was unaccustomed to. He quickly discovered that not only was Algerian home life inaccessible to him, worse still, the Algérienne, even in public but was also concealed from his gaze by virtue of the veil."5

Returning to Alloula, he states, "These veiled women are not only an embarrassing enigma to the photographer but an outright attack upon him." How did French photographers overcome this hurdle?

The photographer will respond to this quiet and almost natural challenge by means of a double violation: he will unveil the veiled and give figural representation to the forbidden." To hell with liberty, equality, and fraternity, he would take "symbolic revenge upon a society that continues to deny him any access and questions the legitimacy of his desire." "History knows of no other society in which women have been photographed on such a large scale to be delivered to public view." states Malek Alloula. The French had "unveiling" campaigns during the Algerian War (1954 -1962) under the pretext of "liberating women." One of the many sinister purposes of these campaigns, much like the brothels and rapes committed by French soldiers, was to demoralise Algerian society, in particular Algerian Muslim men.

Franz Fanon illustrates how forcibly removing Muslim women's hijabs was part of the strategy to crush the Muslim resistance will: "The officials of the French administration in Algeria committed to destroying the people's originality, and under instructions to bring about the disintegration, at whatever cost, of forms of existence likely to evoke a national reality directly or indirectly, were to concentrate their efforts on the wearing of the veil." [6]

It seems that for modern-day imperialists, bad habits die hard. In 2002 George Bush declared to the United Nations General Assembly, "Respect for women... can triumph in the Middle East and beyond!". "The repression of women [is] everywhere and always wrong!"[7] he told the New York Times, suggesting that the west should wage war on Iraq for the sake of its women. The US-led coalition bombed Afghanistan, massacring 240,000 Afghans and 70,000 Pakistanis[8] all in the name of female emancipation. Despite raining hell upon the lives of millions of innocent civilians and irreversibly destroying the economic and social infrastructure of Afghanistan, George Bush and his wife Laura Bush appeared far more moved by tales of Afghans being tortured for wearing nail varnish.

Just like Lord Cromer, Bush employed the language of western feminist discourse to denounce the indigenous culture. The Egyptian feminist and academic Leila Ahmed details how feminism served as a "handmaid to colonialism...Whether in the hands of patriarchal men or feminists," she writes, "The ideas of western feminism essentially functioned to morally justify the attack on native societies and to support the notion of comprehensive superiority of Europe."[9] Although Ahmed inaccurately writes about orthodox Islam in a disparaging manner, her critique of feminism as a colonial tool is factually correct.

Feminism and colonialism have a long and duplicitous history in the Muslim world. Liberal feminists, in general, never support Muslim women's right to obey their Creator. They champion our causes only when we use their language. "My body my choice" has become the mantra of women's liberation, even consciously employed by veiled Muslim women. It's true in all aspects of life, we have a choice whether we obey or disobey our Creator, and we will have to eternally live with the consequences of those decisions in the next life.

Nowadays, Islam has become a celebration, not of commandments, but of choice and individual interpretations of rules. Eeman Abbasi aptly summed up this thinking in her article, *Not My Body Not My Choice,* "Post-Enlightenment liberalism and secularism have made Choice a false God....Many Muslims invoke the Quranic verse that states there is "no compulsion in the religion" (2:256) as justification for their choice of which Islamic injunctions to honour and which to abandon. This complete misreading of the text is dangerous as it creates a liberty of conscience that allows individuals to construct their own religion and tailor their actions not by Divine authority, but by their own whims. It also ignores the remainder of the verse, which reads: "The right course has become clear from the wrong. So whoever disbelieves in *Taghut* and believes in Allah has grasped the most trustworthy handhold with no break in it."[10]

In addition, this reasoning has given rise to the oft-repeated argument, "No one should tell a woman what to wear". This statement is very simplistic. It pretends that women make their clothing choices completely independently, devoid of outside influences such as their social media feeds, friends, adverts, fashion trends, societal rules, and expectations. As believers, Allah and His Messenger (saw) have the right to tell us what to wear. In the Hadith Nawawi, the Prophet (saw) said:"Verily, Allah the Almighty has laid down fara'id (religious obligations), so do not neglect them. He has set boundaries, so do not overstep them. He has prohibited some things, so do not violate them; about some things, He was silent, out of compassion for you, not forgetfulness, so seek not after them."

Allah, in His wisdom, has also instructed parents to teach their children to obey Allah's laws. As narrated by Abdullah Ibn Umar, The Prophet (saw) said: "Indeed each of you is a shepherd, and each of you will be questioned regarding his flock. The commander who is in authority over people is responsible, and he will be questioned regarding his responsibility. The man is responsible for the inhabitants of his house, and he is the one who will be questioned about them. The wife is responsible for her husband's house, and she will be questioned about it. The servant is responsible for his master's property, and he will be questioned about it. Indeed, each of you is a shepherd, and each of you will be questioned about his flock." (Sahih al-Bukhari)

Therefore in Islam, family members can advise and correct each other when they see their loved ones choosing to disobey Allah.

Unfortunately, we have been indoctrinated into accepting that we will only truly be happy when we are autonomous and break free from our religion and family. However, Allah reminds us: "But perhaps you hate a thing, and it is good for you, and perhaps you love a thing, and it is bad for you. And Allah Knows, while you know not." (2:216)

In conclusion, it is clear both modern-day colonialists and their predecessors understood the importance of Muslim women as vanguards of Islam. Now that we know what the colonists did to force our foremothers to remove their hijabs, it should motivate us to hold on even more tightly to our own in the 21st century. History teaches us that knowledge is power. This knowledge of our past will prevent us from being fooled by the enemies of Islam in the present. As the Prophet (saw) said, "A believer is not bitten from the same hole twice." (Bukhari/ Muslim)

Hands Off Our Hijab

"And let them draw their head-coverings (khumur) over their necks and chest (juyoob)..." (An-Nur: 31)

TIME TO PLAY OFFENCE AGAINST THE ANTI-HIJAB SQUAD

A couple of months ago, I had the most surreal conversation with a Muslim feminist 'intellectual'. With absolute conviction, she was trying to convince me that donning the hijab was not compulsory in Islam. Initially, I was bewildered. Had I entered the Twilight Zone? Together with a very patronising tone, this feminist Muslim woman misconstrued the Arabic language in an attempt to deceive me of the true meanings of the Qur'an. Thank God I had researched the topic myself or her arguments might have convinced me. However, for a layperson who may not know Arabic or has little knowledge of the Islamic precepts regarding hijab, it's easy to be convinced by so-called Muslim intellectuals, especially when they evoke meritorious credentials, such as a master's degree in Islamic Law from well-known western institutions.

Let's cut to the chase and call a spade a spade. The anti-hijab squad are mainly progressive Muslims who want to reform Islam. Progressive Muslims identify as Muslims but discard Islam's fundamental tenets and practices because they are inconsistent with their polemics. They are a brand of reformists, proselytising "alternatives" to rules and contesting indisputable axioms of Islam that have 1400 years of scholarly consensus as well as firm evidence from the Qur'an and Prophetic traditions. In addition to their blatant aversion to the hijab, they are pro-LGBTQI+, promote interfaith marriages and claim that women can lead mixed congregational prayers. Here are just a few examples of public statements made by progressives: "I think Shariah [law] is totally made up. "It's not like there's a page in the Qur'an that says, 'For you to be Muslim, you have to live by these set of rules." Ani Zonneveld, Muslims for Progressive Values.[11]

"Today, in the 21st century, most mosques around the world, including in the United States, deny us, as Muslim women, our Islamic right to pray without a headscarf," Asra Nomani, Nomani cofounder of Muslim Reform Movement. Asra Nomani, a self-described Muslim reformer, has supported policies that target Muslims as suspects based on their religious identity. In 2012, Nomani stated she was "relieved that our country's largest police agency was monitoring our Muslim community,"[12]

Moreover, radical feminists and self-appointed saviours like the Egyptian-American writer Mona Eltahawy have taken it upon themselves to be the mouthpiece of secular liberalism in the Middle East and the global Muslim community. Ironically, Eltahawy accomplishes the very thing she accuses Islamic patriarchy of denigrating the autonomy and choices of Muslim women. "I support banning the face veil everywhere and not just in France, where they are to vote on a resolution and possibly a ban on wearing the garment in public places... "[13] Mona Eltahawy is a liberal and describes herself as "a secular, radical feminist Muslim."[14]

A further example is that of Amina Wadud, an American professor and proponent of Islamic feminism: "I have recognised and lived the idea that hijab is a public declaration of identity with Islamic ideology. I do not consider it a religious obligation, nor do I ascribe to it any religious significance or moral value per se. It is certainly not the penultimate denotation of modesty."[15]. Amina Wadud has also openly advocated "pluralism" and "equality" as an endorsement of LGBTQI+ rights.

In an article titled, *As a Muslim feminist, I know what shariah really means - and it's not what the Taliban thinks*, Hafsa Lodi asserts, "Shariah is continuously open to revision, according to numerous religious scholars."[16] The question arises as to why Lodi, a journalist who is supposed to be unbiased, only makes reference to the works of liberal progressive authors and activists such as Mustafa Akyol, Abdullahi Ahmed An-Na'im, Leila Ahmed, Ziba Mir Hosseini and Amina Wadud. She disregards the views of any mainstream Muslim scholars or academics; a tactic used all too often by non-Muslim journalists eager to find so-called independent voices in Muslim academia. This support reveals an attempt to undermine Islamic practices and take advantage of the general ignorance of Islamic legal principles to advance an anti-hijab position. Many governments support such narratives in the west as part and parcel of an agenda to reform Islam. So should we listen to the opinions of progressive Muslims regarding hijab? Are they practising Islam correctly? Yasir Qadhi, the dean of academic affairs at Al-Magrib Institute, points out, "The very fact that the movement is so small or marginal speaks volumes about their sway and influence," says Qadhi, "Let's look at the text of the Qur'an and see what Allah and his messenger want us to do rather than to project our ideas onto the text," Qadhi says.

InshaAllah, I will now explain the scholarly, mainstream Islamic opinions regarding the hijab. Consensus has always existed amongst the sahaba (companions of the Prophet) and classical scholars that wearing a headcover (khimar) and loose outer garment (jilbab) is obligatory. It is only in recent times that the precept of hijab has come under scrutiny as attempts to recast Islam in a liberal image. The following are primary evidences from the Quran and Sunnah regarding the compulsory nature of the hijab as mentioned in the following verse:

"And tell the believing women to reduce [some] of their vision and guard their private parts and not expose their adornment except for what is apparent and let them draw their head covers over their chests and not expose their adornment except to their husbands, their fathers, their husbands' fathers, their sons, their husbands' sons, their brothers, their brothers' sons, their sisters' sons, their women, that which their right hands possess, or those male attendants having no physical desire, or children who are not yet aware of the private aspects of women. And let them not stamp their feet to make known what they conceal of their adornment. And turn to

Allah in repentance, all of you, O believers, that you might succeed." (Surah Nur 24:31)

Let's try to understand this verse and what it is asking us to do. Ibn Kathir in his tafsir said, "It is possible that Ibn Abbas and those who followed him intended by the explanation of the verse, "Except for what is apparent," (24:31) to mean the face and the hands, and this is the well-known opinion among the majority."

Urwah reported: Aisha, may Allah be pleased with her, said, "May Allah have mercy on the foremost women of the Muhajirun. When Allah revealed the verse, 'let them draw their head covers over their chests' (24:31) they cut their sheets and veiled themselves with them." Ṣaḥiḥ al-Bukhari

Aisha reported: Asma' bint Abi Bakr entered the house of the Messenger of Allah (saw) while she was wearing a thin garment, and she showed it to him. The Prophet said, "O Asma, when a woman reaches the age of maturity, it is not proper for her to show anything but this and this," and the Prophet pointed to his face and hands. Sunan Abi Dawud.

The following verse is in relation to the command of wearing loose outer garments: "O Prophet, tell your wives and your daughters and the women of the believers to bring down over themselves their outer garments. That is more suitable that they will be known and not be abused. And ever is Allah Forgiving and Merciful." (Surah Ahzab 33:59)

The meaning of "To bring down over themselves their outer garments (jalabeeb)" indicates that women should cast their outer garments over their persons. To lower the covering means to let it drape down. The jilbab is a cover (milhafah) used to conceal a dress and other items of clothing. It is stated in the al-Qamus al-Muheet (The Arabic Dictionary *Al-Qāmūs al-Muḥīṭ* was compiled by Muḥammad b. Ya'qūb al-Fayrūzābādi (d. 817 AH) that the jilbab is in the form of the (sirdāb) or the (sinmār), which is the gown or a loose garment for women, or that which conceals her clothing like a cover (milhafah). Al-Jawhari stated in as-Sihah (another dictionary) that the jilbab is the cover (milhafah) and some say it is a sheet (mula'ah). There are differences amongst the ulema about the length of the jilbab, and how far should it 'drape' but not about the necessity of a loose-fitted outer garment when a woman is in public.

It has been narrated on the authority of Umm Atiyyah (ra): "We were ordered to bring out our menstruating women and veiled women in the religious gatherings and invocation of Muslims on the two 'Eid festivals. These menstruating women were to keep away from prayer, witnessing the blessing and call to the Muslims. I asked: "Oh Messenger of Allah! What if one of us does not have a jilbab?" He said, "Let her wear the jilbab of her sister." (Muslim)

This means that she did not have a garment to wear over her clothes to go out in, so the Prophet (saw) ordered her to borrow one from her sister. The verse clarifies that Allah (swt) has commanded the Prophet (saw) to tell his wives and the wives and daughters of the Muslims to loosen their garments worn over their clothes which drape down.

The obligatory nature of the Islamic dress code has been confirmed by the statements of the men and women at the time of the Prophet (saw) and by centuries of scholarship, from Imam Nawawi, Ibn Manzur, and Ibn Hazm, to contemporary scholars including Dr Haifaa Younis, Sheikh Nuh Keller, Sheikh Faraz Rabbani, Ustadha Maryam Amir, Shaykh Mohammad Akram Nadwi, Dr Shadee Elmasry, Ustadha Fatima Barkatulla and Imam Omar Suleiman.

Inshaallah, I will now present a series of arguments countering the views against wearing the hijab.

1. **The Arabic word 'hijab' is not mentioned in surah 24:31. The term 'hijab' means a screen, not a headcover. Therefore, women do not have to wear hijab.**

Allah says in the Quran: "And when you ask (his wives) for anything you want, ask them from behind a screen (hijab)." (Al Ahzab:53). It's true in the Quran that the word hijab does not mean headcover. The literal meaning of the word hijab in Arabic is a curtain. It also means hiding, obstructing and isolating someone or something. In the past, the Arabs did not use the word hijab when referring to the headcover. In modern times it has become synonymous with headcover, and we all use it now. So it is correct to say it was never historically used to describe the cloth to cover the hair.

So how do we know we have to cover our heads? Allah says: "And let them draw their head-coverings (khumur) over their necks and chest (juyoob)." (An-Nur: 31) Khumur is the plural of khimar, and it is used to cover the head. Juyoob is the plural of jayb. It is the v-neck opening of a garment, often translated as bosom but encompassing the chest and collarbone area. Thus, Allah (swt) ordered that the khimar be worn over the head and around the neck and chest. So, Allah uses 'khimar' in the Quran, not hijab, to instruct us to cover our heads. The khimar is, in other words, what we now describe as 'hijab'.

2. The word used in surah 24:31 is 'khimar', but that is open to interpretation. It does not mean headcover. The term 'khimar' means shawl. So how do we know khimar is a headcover?

The root word of khimar is kha ma ra: to cover. Khamr (wine) is called such because it covers the human intellect. In the first Arabic dictionary written in 170 H by al-Khalil Ibn Ahmad, there we can find the term *Mukhammarah* which means goat or sheep, specifically a that has a white head. It is said that it is a black goat with a white head. The word khimar linguistically means a covering of the head. It was used to describe such a covering before Islam, and the word has been used to describe the head covering of men. It was one of the names for their turban if it was extra-long and went down to the middle of the belly.

Umm Salamah reported that: The Prophet used to wipe over the shoes and khimar. (Muslim) Ibn Manzoor comments: she meant the "turban" because a man covers his head with it as a woman does the same by her khimar. It is reported that when one of the daughters of the Prophet (saw) died, he was handing them the clothes to wrap her. The hadith says: Then he gave us the Der'a (shirt) followed by the khimar (head cover) then the malhafah (The last piece to wrap the entire body) (Ahmad & Abu Dawood)

The Prophet (saw) said: "Allah does not accept the prayer of any woman who menstruates unless (she wears) a khimar (head cover)." [What is meant by a "woman who menstruates" here is a woman who has reached the age of menstruation, not a woman who has her menses.]

A pre-Islamic style of head covering worn by women was a long cloth tied like a bandana, and then the remaining material would be draped behind their backs. That was also called a khimar. The Quran instructed women to take their khimar and throw it in front of them over their chests. "And let them draw their head-coverings (khumur) over their necks and v-necks (juyoob)." (An-Nur: 31)

The words and sentences of the Qur'an are interpreted according to their linguistic and shariah meanings Thus, it is incorrect to interpret them in any other way. Only a qualified scholar of the Quran, man or woman, can interpret and explain the meaning of ayat. But even they are bound by the linguistic definitions of the words, as the Qur'an was revealed in Arabic.

A layperson cannot take the words of the Qur'an and attempt to translate them in a way that contradicts the precise linguistic meanings of terms, let alone build an argument based on English translations. Samina Ali did this in her TEDx talk, *What does the Quran really say about a Muslim woman's hijab?* She attempted to argue that the word 'khimar' simply means to cover and not to cover the head, which as I have explained above, is not accurate. The question, then, is why didn't Allah (swt) explicitly mention the words' hair' or 'head' in the ayah? This is precisely why claiming the word simply means 'cover' is problematic. The word khimar describes a specific type of cover, the one that covers the hair. In the same way, a 'sock' in the English language is known to be a cover for the feet.

Here are just a few of the skills and knowledge a person must have before they can derive a ruling from an ayah of the Qur'an a person must know:

1. Classical Arabic linguistics, which is the language of the Quran.
2. The fundamental rules concerning the principles of the theory of Islamic law.

3. Knowledge of the Quran methodology in permission, prohibition, obligation and enforcement.
4. The hadith related to that issue.
5. Consideration of the linguistic meaning and the various contexts where a word was mentioned.

Deriving rules from the Quran and sunnah is a specialism and requires years of study like any other specialism. Taking one English translation of an ayah in isolation and ignoring all the other ayat and hadith relating to a topic is a misleading and deceitful method of deriving an Islamic rule.

3. Male scholars have interpreted the ayah and hadith about the hijab. Their interpretations are outdated, and we need women to interpret them instead in the modern context.

The myth that Muslim men have conspired to silence the voices of Muslim women needs to be discussed. Firstly, the gender of a hadith narrator or scholar is irrelevant. Secondly, to disprove the myth, the majority of the evidences related to women covering was narrated by female sahabi such as Aisha (ra) the wife of the Prophet, Zainab (ra), Umm Salama (ra), and they are the ones who conveyed how women interpreted the ayah and hadith in their daily actions. We are not obeying men or male scholars when we cover; we are obeying Allah. Here are just a few examples.

Allah reveals the verse for women to veil. Urwah reported: Aisha, may Allah be pleased with her, said, "May Allah have mercy on the foremost women of the Muhajirun. When Allah revealed the verse, 'Let them draw their cloaks over their bodies,' (24:31) they cut their sheets and veiled themselves with them." Source: Ṣaḥīḥ al-Bukhārī 4481

Muslim women should only reveal their face and hands in front of non-mahram men. Aisha reported: Asma' bint Abi Bakr entered the house of the Messenger of Allah (saw) while she was wearing a thin garment, and she showed it to him. The Prophet said, "O Asma, when a woman reaches the age of maturity, it is not proper for her to show anything but this and this," and the Prophet pointed to his face and hands. Also, throughout Islamic history, female companions and female scholars were all active in the field of gaining knowledge and teaching it to men and women.

The following book illustrates this point al-Muhaddithat: the women scholars in Islam by Mohammad Akram Nadwi. This book is an adaptation in English of the introductory volume of a 40-volume biographical dictionary (in Arabic) of women scholars of the

Prophet's hadith. Learned women enjoyed high public standing and authority in the formative years of Islam. For centuries after that, women travelled intensively for religious knowledge and routinely attended the most prestigious mosques and madrasas across the Islamic world. Typical documents (like class registers and ijazahs from women authorising men to teach) and glowing testimonies about their women teachers from the most revered ulema are cited in detail.

Historically, women played a pivotal role in the foundation of many Islamic educational institutions

- Fatima al-Fihri's founding of the University of Al Karaouine in 859 CE.
- Many female jurists existed. Fatima bint Alauddin al-Samarkhandi (d. 587 AH) was a jurist.
- Dr Faridah Zamarrud, a female scholar of Tafsir/ Morocco.

- Zayn al-Nisa` bint 'Alamkir (1048-1113 h). She was the daughter of king' Alamkir of India, and had a complete tafsir of Qur'an called Zayn al-Tafasir.
- Dr Aisha Abdul Rahman (Bint Al-Shati) wrote a tafsir.

Saying that women had never interpreted the Quran does not reflect a thorough or honest study of Islamic literature. Lastly, the point about juristic interpretation is that it's a discipline to seek Allah's verdict upon a matter without preconceptions. A scholar would be found out in the well-established Islamic process of 'peer review' if he was found to be deducing rules to confirm pre-determined biases.

4. Islam is outdated and must be modernised

One of the most cliched criticisms against Islam is that rulings revealed hundreds of years ago can have little impact on our lives in the 21st century. This has to be addressed. The wearing of the khimar is a religious duty and a means of ibadat. Like all ibadat, it is aimed at worshipping and revering our Creator. Worship does not change through time and place. We wouldn't argue that salah, fasting, and charity need reforming so why do we claim hijab does?

"I support banning the face veil, everywhere and not just in France where they are to vote on a resolution and possibly a ban on wearing the garment in public places…Mona Eltahawy"

Hands Off Our Hijab

CRITIQUING HEAD-SCARVES AND HYMENS BY MONA ELTAHAWY

The women's liberation movement was initiated by non-Muslim, secular, liberal women who believed that women should have 'equal rights' as men. These rights were essentially conceived and devised by John Locke, a 17th-century philosopher and the founding father of liberalism. He states that man is born with natural rights that cannot be taken away. They are the right to life, liberty and property. These rights reflect that all human beings are born equal, in the sense that each individual is of equal moral worth. As each century has passed, these rights have evolved and changed, and so has the feminist movement. Additional rights have been added to this "inalienable rights" list, now known as human rights.

Mona Eltahawy is a liberal and describes herself as "a secular, radical feminist Muslim."[17] Because of this, she looks at the world through the lens of Western interpretations of equality and freedom instead of Islam. Here is a common mistake that I have been guilty of making, and maybe you have too. Muslim women write so few books about Muslim women's issues, so when we see one, we do not evaluate or critique the ideas they are conveying to the extent that we would had a non-Muslim written it. Yet as Muslims, we should seek knowledge and unearth the truth.

I aimed to evaluate her opinions without positive or negative bias. Just because she is a Muslim woman doesn't mean we unquestionably embrace her. Instead, I aimed to assess her views objectively. Moreover, it's essential to determine whether a writer's views align with the majority, scholarly, mainstream Islamic opinions.

Eltahawy's book is written to challenge. She does not mince her words. Like other feminists from the Muslim world, she surmises that Arabs hate women. Her remedy leaves little room for doubt: unless women in the Middle East dispense with religion and their cultures and embrace liberal equality, they will remain mere chattel. Her language is often unpleasant and crude, as she declares, "I believe in the power of profanity…profanity – especially delivered by women – is a powerful way to transgress the red lines of politeness and niceness that the patriarchy."[18] In her mind, that is how she is going to get heard. Women's rights can only be secured after women go through a sexual revolution, dispense with anachronistic norms, and embrace liberal 'modernity.'

Before critiquing her approach, I would like to begin this review with overlaps between my thinking and hers. Regardless of the quality of evidence she cites and the accuracy of her experiences, I agree with her point that the Muslim world is a mess. Women are treated horrifically in many countries, and the injustice many women have to face, coupled with the failure of Arab and Muslim governments to protect their rights, should make us all feel a sense of sadness. The problem is two-fold: firstly, the treatment of women falls short of any sense of a just society, and secondly, the rule of law is non-existent. In other words, very few perpetrators of harm against women seem to face punishment.

I first came across her work when I read the chapter she penned, "Too Loud, Swears Too Much and Goes Too Far", in the troubling book, *It's Not About the Burqa*, where she explains her perspective. She calls for "social and sexual revolutions alongside the political revolutions of the Arab Spring to liberate women from all forms of oppression." Many young Muslim women embrace her views and, of course, are championed by westerners eager to find so-called independent voices in the Muslim world, even if she is a New Yorker.

Achieving social, political, and sexual equality for women is Eltahawy's mission. If she finds an Islamic rule that disagrees with these principles, then this rule has to be rejected. Her connection with Allah is not one of submitting to His omniscience but only to incorporate aspects of the religion that accord with social liberalism. She says, "I insist on the right to critique both my culture and my faith in ways that I would reject from an outsider... I am not naïve enough to think that 'fornication' will disappear as a concept or as a sin from either the Muslim or Christian way of life in our region. I am instead calling for a pragmatic approach to sexuality that would allow consenting adults who choose to have sex with other consenting adults the freedom to do so, with the knowledge and birth control they require to do so safely. That freedom to choose will not infringe on the freedom to decide to wait until marriage if that is what you want. The more freedom we have, the more choices available to people. The fewer freedoms we have, the faster hypocrisy will eat away at the heart of our society."[19]

I genuinely believe many Muslim and non-Muslim women are unhappy about how progressively promiscuous our societies are becoming. There are several books and articles about the Sexual Revolution during the 1960s and its subsequent effects. The Sexual Revolution was a movement that challenged traditional gender norms and called for sexual liberation and equality for women. With it came the normalisation of sex outside of heterosexual, monogamous relationships, increased use of contraception and the pill, pornography, homosexuality, the legalisation of abortion, public nudity, etc.

Unlike first-wave feminism, which focused mainly on legal obstacles to gender equality, liking voting and property, second-wave feminism included "politics, work, the family, and sexuality".[20] The consequence was that women were now positively encouraged to be sexually free and equally promiscuous as men. This view of sex and relationships has been exported globally via popular culture through music, movies, novels and social media. Of course, Muslim countries have not been immune to this proselytisation.

However, this lifestyle goes against Islamic values, normalises *zina*, encourages people to question the sanctity of marriage and promotes shamelessness which in the Quran is called both *al fahsha* and *al fahisha* – lewdness, indecency, vulgarity, or anything inappropriate and ugly.

"And do not approach unlawful sexual intercourse. Indeed, it is ever an immorality and is evil as a way." (Quran 17:32)

Bearing Islamic sexual ethics in mind, it is difficult to understand why the author is advocating quite vociferously for the need for a sexual revolution in Muslim countries.

Eltahawy denounces conservative interpretations of Islam. Maybe here she has a point: Muslim scholars have adopted a conservatism to respond to liberal degradation as a result of two centuries of liberalisation. It's a defensive mechanism to attempt to safeguard the family in the face of a cultural onslaught. However, one must not be under any illusion; if she was offered a selection of more 'softer' Islamic opinions, she would no doubt find any law that didn't accord with a western conception of rights to be unacceptable. A husband seeing it as his responsibility to pay the bills or separate entrances to a mosque would be seen as the patriarchy. She says, "In Tunisia, polygamy was banned, and I agree with this. A man should not be able to marry four women unless a woman can marry four men. I am not monogamous; I don't believe in monogamy, and I don't have just one partner, but Islam allows men to be polygamous and not me. It's unfair. Either both can have multiple partners, or neither can."

The most worrying problem with Eltahawy is that she will not accept an Islam that isn't chastened by secular liberalism. She sounds like a radical, but only in tone. Her prescriptions are as old as the imperialism she borrows them from. Like Lord Cromer before her, the 19th Century Englishman saw women's liberation to be the key to unlocking the Muslim world. In practice, imperialism had a more sinister aim: to destroy the Muslim family as a means to destroy Muslim society.

Name me an Arab country, and I'll recite a litany of abuses against women occurring in that country, abuses fuelled by a toxic mix of culture and religion that few seem willing to disentangle lest they blaspheme or offend. Her solution to the abuse Muslim women face is that Islam must be reformed, and Muslims should take a secular approach to their religion just as some Christians and Jews have. Allah and His Messenger ﷺ come after Locke and Voltaire – for example, supporting the right[21] of newspapers to slander the Prophet ﷺ and that the cartoons "didn't offend"[22] her.

Her criticism of Islam comes in the form of a straw man. She glosses over two centuries of colonialism in the Muslim world, the cause behind despotism and failed societies in Saudi Arabia and Egypt, and instead shifts the blame onto Islam. A true academic would have analysed the status of Muslim women throughout Islamic history, measured that with the decline from the 19th century onwards and the systematic way colonialism and liberalisation contributed to undermining the fabric of Muslim life.

For example, the Saudi family has used religion to maintain the monarchy and justify their autocratic rule. This relationship between religion and monarchy resulted from an 18th-century pact between Muhammad bin Saud [23] and the local religious authority to fight the Ottoman Empire. This pact served and was supported by the British, as it sought to undermine Ottoman strength.

Eltahawy's biggest criticisms are made at Egypt, when an article in the Egyptian criminal code says that if a woman has been beaten by her husband 'with good intentions,' no punitive damages can be obtained, then to hell with political correctness. Egypt is not, by any stretch, a state obedient to Islamic law. Egypt was ruled and shaped by a foreign imperial power: the British Empire. Modern Egypt dates back to 1922 when it gained independence from the

British Empire. However, the British military occupation of Egypt continued. The current prime minister, Abdel Fattah el-Sisi's government, is dedicated to maintaining Egypt as a secular state. This secular state was consolidated by the British to serve their interests. The absence of rights isn't due to Islam, but because of Islam's absence in state and society.

Most secular autocrats in the Muslim world have tried to force liberalisation from above, beginning under colonial powers. Mohammed bin Salman is doing that right now in Saudi, and Hosni Mubarak did this in Egypt. What we have now in the Muslim world are postcolonial constructs that serve Western interests, dysfunctional societies that are failing both men and women.

Liberal elites under autocrats have lived a safe life of luxury. They raid the country of its wealth and flout their social cultures in public, looking down with disdain at the poor and religious. They write books calling for an Islamic reformation, and Muslims that live on a diet of social media outrage find a cause in Eltahawy.

She denies that she wants "the West to rescue us" and that "Only we can rescue ourselves." But after reading this book, it's clear her aim is for Muslim women to replace our Islamic identity and rescue ourselves by adopting her secular liberalism. Her intentions are illustrated by her comments about wearing the hijab and the niqab.

"I support banning the face veil, everywhere and not just in France where they are to vote on a resolution and possibly a ban on wearing the garment in public places…"[24]

What is the difference between what she is saying and the language we have become accustomed to in newspapers and talk shows? The Muslim world is in turmoil, but not because of Islam, but because of its absence. To help Muslim women, we first have to assert our *Islamic* rights in Muslim societies.

Hands Off Our Hijab

"Allah does not look at your appearance or your possessions; but He looks at your heart and your deeds."

(Muslim)

Hands Off Our Hijab

MATERIAL GIRLS

Modest fashion : it's a goldmine. According to the Global Islamic Economic Report, women's modest fashion accounted for $44 billion in sales in 2015. By 2025, it's estimated to be worth $88bn [25] and shows no signs of abating. These figures reveal why global brands want to get their hands on our hijabs! Gucci and Nike have been marketing hijabs since 2018. Dolce & Gabbana launched a lavish collection of abayas back in 2016. And in 2019, Sports Illustrated surprisingly showcased burkinis declaring, "whether you are wearing a one-piece, a two-piece, or a burkini, you are the pilot of your own beauty." Their PR peddles individuality and empowerment, but we know "it's all about the money, money, money". But wait, there's more! In 2021 United Colours Of Benetton launched what is being deemed as a progressive innovation a 'unisex hijab' designed by Italian rap star Ghali.

Modest fashion is a double-edged sword. Sitting writing this in Istanbul: the modest fashion capital of the world (Alhamdulilah), I have no problem finding elegant, full-length dresses and matching scarves. I know it's partly due to the global fashion industry waking up to the lucrative opportunity of modest fashion. Muslimahs no longer have to choose between being fashionable or modest: we can have both. We are proverbially having our cake and eating it.

But can we overlook the not so palatable outcomes of the modest fashion movement? Thirty or so years ago, the term modest fashion didn't exist. If you wanted to wear hijab and jilbab, you would either make it yourself, buy them from an Islamic shop (or Tie Wrack) or get them from a Muslim country. Your options were limited, and to be honest, being fashionable was not the priority: obeying Allah was. We knew there was a time and place to be attractive and gorgeous, and that was in the private sphere. Veteran hijabis look back at that era with nostalgia…

So what was the game changer? Well, it was a combination of hijabi fashion bloggers, Muslim designers, faith-influenced fashion brands and social media. Mainstream brands were neglecting Muslim women, so designers and fashionistas started their own clothing lines, showed women how to style their scarves and adapt clothes to make them adhere to Islamic requirements. Once the big brands realised there were big bucks to be made in modest wear, they opportunistically jumped on the bandwagon.

Today, western brands are the driving force in the modest fashion world. They have hijacked the 'Islamic roots' of modest fashion and replaced it with rampant consumerism, and Muslim women are now their target audience. As targets, we are being stripped away from Islamic influences that may allow us to make rational clothing choices. A 'liberated' woman, an 'autonomous' teenager, are all susceptible to the power of advertisers. Family and religion help us make better decisions - but without these or if you can lessen the influence of a parent or people of knowledge - then left alone, you become a creature of consumption. Halima Aden, the world's first hijab-wearing supermodel, wishes she had listened to her mother's pleas "to open [her] eyes and quit modelling a LONG time ago. I wish I wasn't so defensive,"[26] This is what Durkheim called anomie, the breakdown of structures of guidance and norms.

There is a reason why DKNY, ASOS, and Mango marketers don't use the phrase 'khimar', 'jilbab' or "niqab" in their marketing: it would be a PR disaster. These words have a specific definition in an Islamic framework. In contrast, the term 'modesty' is open to personal interpretation, an expression of individuality: exactly how modern consumer capitalism wants Muslims to view their clothing. So, in essence, our hijab is being reimagined by non-Muslim fashion brands and then aggressively marketed to us.

Modesty is mentioned in the Quranic verses that prescribe hijab: "And say to the believing women that they should lower their gaze and guard their modesty; that they should not display their beauty and ornaments except what must ordinarily appear therof; that they should draw their veils over their bosoms..." (24:31)

But let's not forget, fundamentally, we wear hijab as an act of worship alone solely for the sake of Allah, and inshallah, we will be rewarded for our obedience. No one denies that the Islamic dress code conceals our bodies. But modesty is a relative expression, different for everyone depending on their cultural practice. On the other hand, Islam has defined with precision how and which areas of a woman's body should be covered. Hence, modesty is not the criterion for choosing what we wear: the Shariah is.

Aisha Hasan, the founder of the Qarawiyyin Project notes in the article, People think hijab sexualises young girls because of the Muslim community, "But it would be naïve to not also recognise that many Muslim women have used the idea of modesty alone to dictate how they should dress, arguing that it is the spirit, not the specifics of the Islamic dress-code, that is important."[27]
This idea that we only have to follow the spirit rather than the letter of Islamic law is just plain wrong. If it were correct, then why not apply it to the dietary rules in Islam? This thinking would make drinking wine and pork acceptable.

As mentioned earlier, the fashion industry encourages rampant consumerism and environmentally unfriendly throw-away fashion, which Islam does not condone. The fashion industry thrives on discontent, making us desire what is trending. Islam instructed us to be presentable, but we don't need to overhaul our wardrobe every season. Furthermore, it's sad to see Muslim fashion brands perpetuating the same unrealistic euro centric beauty standards by opting for tall, fair, slim, airbrushed models. I know clothes hang better on thin stick models; I have read The Beauty Myth[28]. But where is the diversity? Why are they using unethical marketing techniques to sell clothing to Muslims? Not only that, we've all heard of the marketing motto "sex sells", and so we are witnessing the blatant sexualisation of hijab and Muslim models on catwalks.

One of the many reasons Halima Aden, cited for quitting runway shows was, "I eventually drifted away and got into the confusing grey area of letting the team on-set style my hijab... I trusted the team on set to do my hijab, and that's when I ran into problems," she said, adding "like jeans being placed on my head in place of a regular scarf...My hijab kept shrinking and got smaller and smaller with each shoot." The former model also spoke about a "horrendous" magazine cover that made her look like a "white man's fetishised version of me". She also said she felt pressure from other Muslim women to "be more daring" and tried "to be the 'hot hijabi' as if that didn't just defeat the whole purpose".[29]

Like sheep to the slaughter, we consume, like and applaud these provocative sexualised images, and perversely we emulate them. Like Muslim models, we are expected to be compliant. Those who do not adopt the modest fashion industry's version of hijab are made to feel frumpy and represent a traditional Islam that has failed to keep up with modernity.

Do you think we may have been a bit too hasty in uncritically embracing the modest fashion movement? Compliant consumers god forbid, fashion victims mesmerised by the allure of being on-trend and garnering compliments for our unique style. What have we lost at the altar of fashion? Are we following in the footsteps of the vain emperor in his new clothes? Have we been persuaded to reject our khimar and jilbabs in exchange for turbans, skinny jeans and individuality?

In January 2023, Batul Bazzi, a famous fashion influencer based in the United States, deleted images from Instagram and TikTok as she no longer wanted to promote content that was not Islam-focused. Batul stated, 'I want to level up with my modesty' and does not want to keep 'promoting an image of myself that does not align with who I am on the inside.' Alhamdulilah, it's heartening to see more and more Muslimahs discarding the 'fashion victim mindset' and embracing an Islamic perspective on fashion.

Today, fashion designers and models have too much influence: Rihanna, Bella Hadid, Kylie Jenner, Calvin Klein etc. are literally worshipped in the west. Secular liberalism encourages people to become obsessed with themselves, their beauty, their bodies their clothes. They are so fixated with the outer appearance because this life means everything. They have no other purpose in life. We don't want to follow in their footsteps. Islam encourages us to be beautiful and stylish but within limits set by our Creator, not His creation.

Abdullah ibn Mas'ud said that the Prophet (saw) said, "No one will enter Paradise who has an atom's weight of pride in his heart." A man said, "What if a man likes his clothes to look good and his shoes to look good?" He said, "Allah is beautiful and loves beauty. Pride means denying the truth and looking down on people." (Muslim)

We must also bear in mind the hadith in Sahih Muslim where the Prophet (saw) said, "Allah does not look at your outward appearance and your wealth, rather He looks at your hearts and deeds."

So, Allah wants us to beautify our tongues with the truth. Our hearts with sincere devotion (ikhlas), love, repentance and obedience. Beautify our bodies by showing His blessings upon us in our clothing. We should recognise Allah through these qualities of beauty and seek to draw close to Him through beautiful words, deeds and attitudes.

In Sunan at-Tirmidhi, it says, "Allah loves to see the effects of His blessing on His slave." It was reported that Abul-Ahwas al-Jashami said the Prophet (saw) saw him wearing old, tattered clothes and asked him, "Do you have any wealth?" I said, "Yes." He said, "What kind of wealth?" I said, "All that Allah has given me of camels and sheep." He said, "Then show the generous blessings that He has given you."

Following the prophetic tradition will help us develop a healthy balanced attitude towards style and spirituality, and reading the tafsir of the ayat regarding clothing will prevent us from compromising our religious beliefs. Inshallah, never forget, my dear sisters: we are slaves of Allah, not slaves to fashion.

"For Muslim men and women,

for believing men and women,

for devout men and women,

for true men and women,

for men and women who are patient and constant,

for men and women who humble themselves,

for men and women who give in charity,

for men and women who fast (and deny themselves),

for men and women who guard their chastity,

and for men and women who engage much in Allah's praise,

for them has Allah prepared forgiveness and great reward."

(33:35)

TOO AFRAID TO WEAR HIJAB?

Some Muslims are telling sisters that it is acceptable not to wear hijab if they fear they will be harassed or if they have been the actual subject of harassment. They argue that if the headscarf causes women to stand out and puts them in the way of harm and if uncovering the head is not considered socially immodest in general society, then it is permissible for Muslim women not to wear the headscarf. They loosely use the principle within Islamic law of (dharura) that "dire need makes what is ordinarily prohibited temporarily permitted." Although this is a well-established principle, we need to understand the rule in detail to ensure we do not misapply it to our circumstances. Just because we face some hostility, we can't assume it's permissible to stop wearing hijab.

Like other requirements of Islam, when wearing hijab, we all experience the natural highs and lows that every believer endures. Every woman's hijab journey is unique, and I'm not judging anyone's worth in the sight of Allah. That is not for me or anyone else to do. The purpose of this discussion is not to judge anyone's intentions or actions. Instead, I want to clarify how we should be reacting to the harassment we face as Muslims. Secondly, I will address how we should correctly apply this Islamic principle of dharura and cope with the confusion and fear we feel due to the behaviour of islamophobes and racists.

Fear is difficult to quantify

Allah says, "And We will surely test you with something of fear and hunger and a loss of wealth and lives and fruits but give good tidings to the patient." (2:155)

Fear is highly subjective. When we feel scared, how can we measure our fear? Are our worries just imagined or legitimate fears? We may ask ourselves, "How do I know if the fear that I feel gives me the ruksa or licence to do things that are ordinarily prohibited? Or to abandon things that are usually an obligation?" For example, we may fear praying salah or saying salam back to someone that greets us, are we allowed to abandon Islam on fear alone?

Understanding dharura in Islam

A principle in Islamic law explains that "dire need makes what is ordinarily prohibited temporarily permitted' for that particular individual. What is considered 'dharura' is an absolute dire need or being forced into a situation of dire need where there is a danger to one's life and limb.

Before we apply this principle to our situation, we must understand what conditions must be fulfilled before we abandon an obligation. To be in a state of dharura individually or collectively is very difficult. We have to accept to a certain extent that when we pray in public or wear hijab, we will face challenges and tests. It is, in fact, a sign of iman to withstand these tests, and the Quran and Sunnah are replete with texts that build our characters to respond to these, "Do the people think that they will be left to say, 'We believe, and they will not be tried?" (29:2)

Islam originally began as a strange phenomenon in society. The idea of worshipping only one God and adhering to universal moral teachings was distasteful to the pre-Islamic Arab society, whose ethics and loyalties were based upon tribalism and idolatry.

After Islam won the hearts and minds of the Arabs and subsequently spread throughout the world, the teachings of Islam were no longer viewed as strange at all. However, the Prophet (saw) warned us that days would come when Islam would return to being odd in society just as it began.

Abu Huraira reported: "The Messenger of Allah, (saw), said: Islam began as something strange, and it will return to being strange, so blessed are the strangers." (Sahih Muslim)

There will be times and places when being a Muslim is challenging, and the mainstream society will shun the teachings of Islam. Muslims will be viewed as weird, troublesome, or even enemies of the state. Yet if we face such trials, we should rejoice because "blessed are the strangers."

We have been duly warned that in some times and places, Muslims will be outcasts of society such that adhering to Islam will be like grasping a hot coal, yet we should find comfort in the fact that such Muslims who remain steadfast in their faith will have their rewards greatly multiplied.

Abu Tha'labah reported: The Messenger of Allah, (saw), said: Verily, ahead of you are days of patience, wherein patience will be like grasping hot coals, and the one who does good deeds will have the reward of fifty men who do likewise. (Sunan Abī Dāwūd)

We have to have a certain level of perseverance with whatever is thrown our way, and hardship does not give us an excuse to abandon our faith and our practice altogether. If that was the case and we could use the principle of 'dharura' to do away with all public aspects of our faith, then Islam would have disappeared in Makkah in the early days of revelation. However, we see in Makkah that the Prophet (saw) and the companions carried out strategic actions -- such as going to the Kaaba and reading the Quran - to display their faith publicly and to show that Islam and Muslims were not going away.

However, not every Muslim was placed in the same situation. Every one of us is not going to be able to contend with the same amount of pressure. Some people live in more complex contexts or more lenient circumstances. When we study the seerah we can see all the Muslims at some point went through some level of emotional or physical difficulty, be that ridicule, verbal abuse, financial hardship or family problems purely because they believed in la illah illal Allah Muhammad rasul Allah. The daughters of the Prophet (saw) Ruqayya and Umm Kulthum were married to the sons of Abu Lahab and were divorced to express animosity towards the Prophet (saw).

So how do we apply the Islamic principle of dharura regarding fear? As I said previously, fear is hard to quantify. The ayat revealed about dharura mainly were concerning food at the time of starvation: "He hath forbidden you only carrion, and blood, and swine flesh, and that which hath been immolated to (the name of) any other than Allah. But he who is driven by necessity, neither craving nor transgressing, it is no sin for him. Lo! Allah is Forgiving, Merciful" (2:173). The ayah relates to extreme hunger where you have to eat something that is ordinarily haram to eat. It would be misapplied if, for example, we were at an office dinner and to not stand out as different we drank wine.

Verbal Abuse

Is verbal abuse enough to evoke the Islamic permission of dhurura? Firstly, the scholars say harm is of different levels. When it comes to verbal insults and derogatory comments, should we let the ignorant, backward actions of racists and islamophobes dictate to us how we are going to practice our faith? They are modern-day Abu Lahabs and Umm Jameels. Rather let's take our cues from the Prophet (saw). He did not alter his obedience to Allah in the face of hostility from the bigots of Quraish. There is also no guarantee that they will stop abusing you even if you remove your hijab. They also have a problem with Sikh men who wear turbans. For Sikhs, the turban is not about culture but an article of faith that is mandatory for men. Fundamentally, ignorant extremists have a problem with anyone who is different from them.

At what level of fear can I abandon an obligation?
- When the insults reach a level of systemic violence.
- There is a genuine fear for your life because you are a Muslim.
- It becomes a norm, and you have no legal protection, and you will be attacked.

Then that is when the principle of dharura can be acted upon if leaving the place where you are being attacked is impossible. The Islamic rule is that you are obliged to migrate if you can no longer practise your deen. "Was not the earth of Allah spacious [enough] for you to emigrate therein?" (4:97) - Allah will account those that abandoned their faith instead of leaving the land of persecution.

Except those that cannot leave."As for the helpless men, women and children who have neither the strength nor the means to escape, For those, it is expected that Allah will pardon them, and Allah is ever Pardoning and Forgiving. And whoever emigrates for the cause of Allah will find on the earth many [alternative] locations and abundance (4:99-100).

A deplorable modern-day example is the persecution of the Uyghur Muslims. The authoritarian Chinese government monitors, imprisons and tortures Uyghur Muslims who practice Islam publicly. They have no means of escape, and the government forbids them from travelling outside their immediate region. They are in a dire situation, and it is a matter of life and death for them. So, in their case, they are permitted to temporarily leave specific obligatory actions and believe in their hearts.

We have a responsibility to help them and work to remove their suffering. The Prophet (saw) said "You see the believers as regards their being merciful among themselves and showing love among themselves and being kind, resembling one body, so that, if any part of the body is not well then the whole body shares the sleeplessness (insomnia) and fever with it."

We should do dua for our Uyghur brothers and sisters. Raise awareness about their situation via our social media. Donate to charities that are supporting them and attend demonstrations against the Chinese regime.

There were times in Makkah when the Prophet (saw) and the Muslims were attacked. Safety is in the hands of Allah (swt), and we are going to find ourselves in difficult situations, but the norm should be that we can practice our faith. 'Utbah ibn Rabi'ah severely beat Abu Bakr As-Siddiq until he was on the verge of death, even though he was a well-respected member of Makkan society.

Muslims have lived in the west for hundreds of years, and there have always been people who say we should do more to assimilate into the culture we live in. "Don't stand out. Give your kids anglicised names. Don't speak your native language in public". However, are we assuming the worst of the situation? There are real situations of fear, but are we being more insecure than we need to be? Moreover, there are laws against discrimination and harassment in many western countries, so we have to take advantage of the legal protections that exist in the laws of the country we live in.

When it comes to our public displays of faith, we need to measure every context. A condition of the principle of dharura is that you only leave an obligation out of fear of life and limb temporarily to keep yourself safe whilst a threat is imminent. Therefore, we should only do it for the amount of time we absolutely have to do it. So, once the fear and threat of violence have gone, we must return to the obligation. We cannot abandon an obligation permanently.

Fear should not dictate our faith.

We need to recognise that when we insist on practising our faith the way Allah (swt) has commanded us to, and the law of the land protects our right to practice our faith, we are making our communities safer and stronger. In contrast, if each of us abandons our faith publicly because we individually want to feel safer, we make our fellow Muslims who are insisting on following Allah's commands less safe.

When we find ourselves in a state of fear, this is the time to turn to Allah. We need to get closer to Allah and build our connection with Him. "Is it not He (the one) who responds to the distressed one when he calls out to Him?"(Surah Naml 27:62)

That will help us persevere and hold on to our obligations, especially when we do things to please Him for His sake. Ours is a religion of hope. There is always light at the end of the tunnel. We shouldn't listen to the pessimistic voices that are weakening our iman or people who are scaremongering and saying we will be wiped out or interned. Allah (swt) will protect us.

The Prophet (saw) said, "Whoever says the people have perished or the people have no hope, he is the most hopeless of them. In another narration, he said, "He is the one making them hopeless".We must not let fear dictate our faith. When we are courageous and steadfast, Allah will ensure us His protection. On the authority of Abu Abbas Abdullah bin Abbas the Prophet (saw) said,

"Be mindful of Allah, and you will find Him in front of you. Recognise and acknowledge Allah in times of ease and prosperity, and He will remember you in times of adversity. And know that what has passed you by [and you have failed to attain] was not going to befall you, and what has befallen you was not going to pass you by. And know that victory comes with patience, relief with affliction, and hardship with ease." (Tirmidhi) If you have further questions about this topic, please speak to a trustworthy scholar, sheikha or imam.

Hands Off Our Hijab

"Know you not that Allah knows all

that is in heaven and on the earth?"

(22:70)

GOOD HIJABIS SHATTER STEREOTYPES

Once upon a time in the west, it was very unusual to see a woman in a hijab on TV, on the cover of a book, or generally being represented in a positive light. The word 'hijabi' didn't exist back then. So when I began my hijab journey at college in the 90s, it was a pretty lonely one. I was one of the first students to wear hijab and jilbab, so I stuck out like a sore thumb. Fellow students would stop and stare at me, trying to figure out what had got into me, and I'm sure my teachers thought my parents had forced me to cover up. By the way, they didn't. Although it was tough, being one of the most visible Muslims at college was a blessing in disguise. It meant girls who were curious about Islam would come and ask me questions. So it was an unexpected opportunity to do dawah, alhamdulillah! It also dawned on me that when you wear a hijab, people will look to you as a representative of Islam. Whether we like it or not, that is a cross that all hijabis have to bear.

Twenty years on, times have changed. Muslim women donning some type of head cover, i.e. a dupatta, a turban or full hijab, are all over the media. No one can deny that a consensus exists amongst the political establishment, mainstream fashion industry, Hollywood and journalists regarding who is a "good hijabi" deserving a platform and who is a "bad hijabi" and must be sidelined.

So, who is this "bad hijabi" I hear you ask? She dresses traditionally, i.e. khimar and jilbab; therefore, she is labelled frumpy and unfashionable. Halima Aden's mother raised this issue with her daughter when trying to persuade her to leave modelling. A bad hijabi holds non-progressive views about gender roles and family and isn't taken in by feminist rhetoric. Consequently, she's out of touch and is upholding the patriarchy. If she dares to be political and speaks up about the illegal occupation of Palestine, Kashmir or Afghanistan, Emma Barnett won't welcome her on BBC's Woman's Hour. Pertinent cases are Dr. Haifaa Younis and Farhat Hashmi. She has made an effort to learn about her deen, so she's a proud, confident Muslimah: the west's worst nightmare. Ustadah Fatima Barkatulla comes to mind when thinking of such a woman. All these reasons are why she will never adorn the cover of Vogue magazine, be invited to talk shows to speak about Muslim women or win a Nobel Peace Prize.

So who is a good hijabi? The west has constructed stereotypes about Muslim women portraying them as quiet housewives, submissive, covered-up, uneducated and unattractive. Consequently, a good hijabi must shatter these stereotypes. Malala Yousafsai is a classic example of a good hijabi. She is adored by Ellen, Emma Watson, Angelina Jolie, Oprah, Megan Markle, The Obamas and The UN etc. Why is she given wall to wall publicity and soon her own TV show? Because she believes in liberal secular values and promotes them to her target audience: young Muslim women. She seldom criticises western foreign policy in the Muslim world.

Amani Alkhatahtbeh, the founder of www.muslimgirl.com, is another example. Feminists love her because her views align with radical feminism. In an interview with Teen Vogue, she said Millenial Muslimahs should "interpret things in their own way". Inshallah may Allah forgive both our sisters for their mistakes.

You might be thinking, why am I picking on Malala and Amani? Who am I to judge? I don't know their intentions. Let me explain. Both these women are foisted upon us, and we are told they are our role models. They are shattering stereotypes. We should follow their example. They ask us to support them; they say they represent Muslim women. It's true sometimes they do speak up for Muslims. But if we follow them, share their wedding photos, promote their books and donate to their charities. Does that mean we have to passively accept their PR and never question their public actions when they contradict Islam?

Shockingly, in a bid to promote their version of a good hijabi, western governments are pretty happy to spend taxpayers hard-earned money. In 2019 SuperSisters, an online Muslim lifestyle platform aimed at British Muslim teenagers was forced to admit it had covertly been funded by the counter-terrorism programme Building a Stronger Britain Together (BSBT).

SuperSisters was created by J-Go Media and promoted as a "global platform for young Muslimahs in east London to share and create inspiring and empowering content"[30]. But it turns out the directors of the platform were non-Muslims. But wait, there's more! It was deliberately producing content promoting a state-approved version of Islam with the potential to track its target audience of young British Muslim girls.

Sabah Ismail, a social media manager for SuperSisters, resigned her position and told the Guardian newspaper, "despite running a project for Muslim women, most of the team were far removed from the principles of Islam, some even disagreeing out-rightly with our beliefs". Amid producing videos, articles and social media posts, Ismail used religious text quoting the Prophet Muhammad (saw) in content designed for a Muslim audience. One day she turned up to work to find "all that was taken off the site and archived. They said they wanted to do away with anything overtly Islamic". Ismail says she felt "used" as "a female Muslim puppet" to legitimise the project.[31]

Supersisters is not the first time the British government has tried to covertly mould Muslim women's identities. In 2019, the Middle East Eye exposed the media platform, This is Woke, as targeting Muslim youth on behalf of the Office for Security and Counter-Terrorism. They produce liberal progressive content for Muslims, including posts titled "You can be both a feminist and a Muslim" Past projects included videos intended to influence conversations among young British Muslims. Women interviewed for a video "What does wearing a hijab mean to you?" said that they were approached on the School of Oriental and African Studies campus and asked whether they would participate in a film marking International Women's Day. Elif Kalin was one of the participants. "We certainly weren't told that it was anything to do with the Prevent programme."

The purpose of these underhand schemes is to tell us how we should view Islam, who we should take as our role models and redefining our Muslim identity. Alhumdulilah's their plans were exposed by sincere Muslims who could see their confusing content was a mixture of Islam and liberalism. These examples remind us that we shouldn't blindly follow and support a platform because it has Islam or Muslim in the name. We all have to be more discerning, expect a Muslim platform and Muslim public figures to follow Islamic principles, and not be scared of calling out unislamic content.

Interestingly, in the speech Message to the grassroots (1964), Malcolm X (El-Hajj Malik el-Shabazz), who I greatly admire, described two types of black people. One craved acceptance from white people, and the other did not.

"During slavery, you had two Negroes. You had the house Negro and the field Negro...The house Negro (Uncle Tom) usually lived close to his master. He dressed like his master...So whenever that house Negro identified himself, he always identified himself in the same sense that his master identified himself...But then you had another Negro out in the field. The house Negro was in the minority. The masses-the field Negroes were in the majority...The slavemaster took Tom and dressed him well and fed him well and even gave him a little education, gave him a long coat and a top hat and made all the other slaves look up to him. Then he used Tom to control them. The same strategy that was used in those days is used today by the same white man. He takes a Negro, a so-called Negro, and makes him prominent, builds him up, publicises him, makes him a celebrity, and then he becomes a spokesman for Negroes and a Negro leader."

I believe the Muslim community can learn a lot about representation from El-Hajj Malik el-Shabazz's observations about the black community in the US. On a related note, I would highly recommend reading The Autobiography of Malcolm X. I read it when I was eighteen, and it had a profound effect on how I perceived myself as a Muslim living in the west.

It's safe to assume that western governments and media platforms will continue to try and influence Muslim women. Hoping to advance their liberal agenda, selectively presenting "progressive Muslims" to encourage a biased perception of what it means to be a "good hijabi". Our only protection against this manipulative behaviour is to follow Allah's guidance.

"O you who believe, do not take anyone as an insider but those from among your own selves. They would spare no effort to do you mischief. They want you to be in trouble. Malice has come out of their mouths while what is concealed in their hearts is still worse. We have made the signs clear to you, if only you understand." (3:118)

In his tafsir of this ayah, Ibn Kathir wrote, "The hypocrites try their very best to confuse, oppose and harm the believers any way they can, and by using any wicked, evil means at their disposal. They wish the very worst and difficult conditions for the believers."

Allah also says, "Never will the Jews or Christians be pleased with you, until you follow their faith. Say, "Allah's guidance is the only ˹true˺ guidance." And if you were to follow their desires after ˹all˺ the knowledge that has come to you, there would be none to protect or help you against Allah. (2:120)

Al-Tabari (may Allah have mercy on him) said: What is meant by the words "Never will the Jews nor the Christians be pleased with you (O Muhammad صلى الله عليه وسلم) till you follow their religion" is: Neither the Jews nor the Christians will ever be pleased with you, O Muhammad, so stop trying to please them and seek the pleasure of your Lord by calling them to that with which Allaah has sent you of the truth. Tafseer al-Tabari (1/565).

This ayah carries a severe warning to us against imitating the ways and methods of the Jews and Christians; after they have acquired knowledge of the Qur'an and Sunnah, may Allah grant us refuge from this behaviour. Although the speech in this ayah was directed towards the Messenger (saw), the ruling applies to all Muslims.

Hands Off Our Hijab

INDIA & THE HIJAB BAN

On January 1 2022, the startling news broke that the Government PU College for Girls, in Udupi, in the Indian state of Karnataka, refused to let students wearing hijab and niqab attend classes. PU College stated that such clothing reflected a flouting of its dress code and resulted in non-uniformity amongst students. Ironically, the college rulebook specifically mentions hijab as permissible so long as it matches the student's uniform; furthermore, the girls in question had been wearing hijab for over three years while attending the college. The students fearlessly refused to budge and staged a peaceful protest outside the college gates. To show their support for their sisters, Muslim male students also joined the protests and began boycotting classes.

As events unfolded, several other colleges in the district also imposed a hijab ban in retaliation to the protests. Within weeks, like a contagious disease, the discriminatory ban spread from one district to another and even to neighbouring states in just a month. The colleges invoked the principles of secularism, uniformity, equality and nationalism to justify the unwarranted ban. However, the ground reality and public response showed an evident, targeted humiliation and exclusion of Muslim girls. Finding the opportunity ripe, cowardly right-wing Hindus mobilised the very classmates of these hijabi girls to protest against them. Mobs of hate-fuelled Hindu students and right-wing activists showed up at college premises in saffron-clad shawls and turbans- saffron being the colour of Hindutva- driving a false equivalence between hijabs and their saffron scarves.

It was implied that Hindu students were somehow deprived of their religious rights if Muslim students were allowed to display religious symbols. The court made a similar argument that permitting the hijab is equivalent to giving privileges to Muslim students while others are not allowed to observe their religion. However, it is a pretty poor and ridiculous equivalence as the demand of Hindu students was conditional on Muslim women's appearance; they would wear saffron shawls if Muslim girls wore the hijab, and they would abandon it if Muslim girls abandoned their hijabs.

Whereas Muslim women wear hijab irrespective of the presentation of other religions, their practice is not predicated on anyone else's robing or disrobing out of their free will. It should also be noted that another religious minority, Sikhs, who observe the custom of wearing turbans, were not accused of flouting uniform rules. The rigid rules applied only to Muslim students.

The coming days saw several altercations between dauntless Muslim girls and mobs of saffron-clad Hindu fanatics. Lone, minor Muslim girls, were openly mocked by crowds, terrorised by extremist sloganeering as they saw their friends and teachers spinelessly turn their backs on them. The bigoted Hindu students and activists threatened to boycott classes unless the girls were forced to remove their hijab. On February 7, the PU College authorities allowed the girls to return on the condition that they sit in a separate room where no teaching would be provided to them. This is the beginning of an official Islamophobic apartheid system in India.

It should be kept in mind that India has a significant Muslim population numbering over 200 million. It is entirely common for Indian Muslim women to observe purdah, the hijab being the most common among students and working professionals. As such, it was rather odd that a synchronised ban in colleges erupted simultaneously in different locations. It was amply clear that the ban had been pre-meditated and was being orchestrated to harass Muslims maintaining the pattern of aggravated Islamophobia in the last few years.

Islamophobia, India and Muslim Women

A common perception prevails that Islamophobia in India was begotten by the current ruling party of India, the BJP(Bhartiya Janata Party) and its several support organisations, such as the RSS (Rashtriya Swayamsevak Sangh). However, India has a long history of Islamophobia. It was ubiquitous to hear of lynchings of Muslims in broad daylight, pre-election riots and harassment of Muslims even before the BJP regime.

It is difficult to say whether the Islamophobia of the masses fuels the Islamophobic government or the government fuels the Islamophobic masses. The social sentiment among the majority does not depart from the government's. The BJP regime has merely given more impunity to the already prevalent Islamophobia, not invented it. This has indeed led to a spike in unabashed Islamophobia. In the state of Madhya Pradesh, a movement was started to ban the hijab. In Gurugram, Friday jamaat was constantly attacked by Hindu thugs asking to stop namaz in public places. Recently several massive Dharm sansads (religious conferences) were organised in various Indian states, with attendance running into thousands that openly called for arming of Hindu masses to slaughter Muslims.- Taking cognisance of the dharm sansads, Prof Gregory Stanton, the founder of Genocide Watch, who previously predicted the Rwandan genocide, issued an urgent notice on the impending genocide of Indian Muslims. During a US congressional briefing, Stanton said there were early "signs and processes" of genocide in the Indian state of Assam and Indian-administered Kashmir.

"We are warning that genocide could very well happen in India," Stanton explained that genocide was not an event but a series of events and drew parallels between the policies pursued by Indian Prime Minister Narendra Modi and the discriminative policies of Myanmar's government against Rohingya Muslims in 2017.

Among the laws he cited were the cancellation of the special autonomous status of Indian-administered Kashmir in 2019 – which robbed Kashmiris of the special autonomy they had for seven decades – and the Citizenship Amendment Act the same year, which bestowed citizenship to religious minorities but banned Muslims. Stanton fears a similar scenario to Myanmar, where the Rohingya were first legally declared non-citizens and then expelled through violence and genocide. "What we are now facing is a very similar kind of a plot," he said. Stanton said the Hindutva ideology was "contrary to the history of India and the Indian constitution and referred to Modi as an "extremist who has taken over the government".

Historically, Muslims are one of India's most marginalised communities, even before the BJP's electoral win. The fortunate ones among us face systematic marginalisation, discrimination in classrooms and workplaces, and bigotry from colleagues and government officials; the unfortunate among us are publicly lynched or killed in regular anti-Muslim pogroms. In "The Production of Hindu Muslims Violence in Contemporary India", Social scientist Paul Brass wrote that as early as 2003,"…hardly a month passes in India in which a Hindu-Muslim riot does not occur that is large enough to be noted in the press".

Muslims perform poorly on most social indicators, such as average income or representation in government institutions. The literacy rate among Muslims, especially Muslim women, is among the country's lowest. It is common to hear of discrimination against Muslim students even in reputable institutes. The state has left no stone unturned to force Muslims out of education and public life in general. From the scrapping of grants and funds to minority institutions, exclusion of Urdu (medium of education and mother tongue of several low-income Muslim households getting elementary education from madrasahs) from public spaces, policing of eating habits, cow vigilantism to the latest attack on hijab, bigotry against Indian Muslims sits well ensconced within the world's largest secular democracy.

In an OpEd for Al Jazeera, the academic Apoorvanand wrote. "Under BJP's leadership, India became one of the most dangerous countries for Muslims and Christians in the world. They are being persecuted physically, psychologically and economically... "Laws are being passed to criminalise their religious practices, food habits and even businesses." Muslim women's gender and religious intersection make them vulnerable, primarily due to easily identifiable religious markers such as hijab or niqab. Despite that, the active participation of Muslim women in Indian politics with ample backing from the rest of the community seems to have rattled everyone across the political spectrum who has historically painted us as subjugated and voiceless. To justify their bias and force it into a reality, they have applied every tactic possible to move Muslim women into invisibilisation. The ban on hijab in educational institutes of Karnataka is now being used to attack every woman in hijab irrespective of the space. Hijabi women are being stopped at banks and polling booths, abused on roads and on public transport. Even teachers who are not supposed to observe any uniform were made to take off their hijab and abaya at the gates. Several cameramen hid in anticipation of capturing the moment of Muslim women disrobed and upload it on social media.

Another tactic used to insult Muslim women came to the fore towards the end of 2020 when an auctioning app called "Sulli Deals" with pictures and details of several Indian Muslim women went viral. The app sought to put a price on Muslim women and carry out a mock-trafficking scenario to humiliate politically active women. At the beginning of 2022, another app called "Bulli Bai" emerged that yet again aimed to "sell" Muslim women as slaves or charlatans. "Sulli" and "Bulli" are common slurs against Muslim women derived from morphing the term "Mulla", which is commonly used to refer to any Muslim in India. It is a peculiar game of pushing Muslim women into subjugation and humiliation, then playing the saviour by pretending to pull them out of their own imposed oppression.

The Public Debate

Udupi, the location of the genesis of the ban, is an obscure district in Karnataka, and the incident wouldn't have garnered attention had independent Muslim news portals and journalists not actively reported and publicised the incident. The power of social media should not be underestimated in Indian politics. The boon for the political propagandist paid IT cell members of various political parties; it has occupied a central space in socio-political developments. Even a cursory glance at the popular sentiment on domains like Twitter and Facebook presents a dismal situation. The case for the struggle for minority rights was very soon reduced to fallacious debates about seemingly progressive ideas like secularism and feminism from the liberal majority. The demand for unconditional support has been overlooked to date.

Ironically, according to self-proclaimed saviours, the case for "liberating" oppressed women is to deprive us of education and a career. Minor Muslim girls wishing to study with a hijab are being equated to mobs of Hindu right-wing activists willing to impose majoritarian customs and hamper public law and order. A pseudo-debate laced with progressive language has been propped up to avoid the discussion on the religious rights of minorities.

Moreover, the liberal, "cultural Muslims" have leveraged their Muslim names and background to support the idea of the non-essentiality of the hijab. Such elite Muslims have ulterior motives in speaking against the community as they hold most positions of nominal representations in mainstream media as palatable, "good and moderate" Muslims. Their consistent stance of chiding other Muslims and their regressive practices helps cement themselves as the ultimate image of what a Muslim is and can be. Any public perception of a Muslim different from them, such as hijab-wearing practising Muslim women, threatens the careers of these elite, liberal media representatives of Muslims. They match the islamophobes in opposing the hijab and give the opposition a Muslim angle.

Essential Religious Practices

The most popular public rhetoric has been that 'Hijab is not an "essential religious practice" in Islam'; hence Muslim girls shouldn't insist on following non-obligatory practices. The Essential Religious Practices ('ERP') test holds that Articles 25 and 26 of the Indian constitution only protect religious practices that are essential or integral to the religion. Decide the grounds for claiming the protection of religious beliefs, the extent of permissible state intervention and overriding exceptions to the right to freedom of religion.

The recent verdict on the hijab gives rise to many questions about the practices of minorities and defining of religious essentials and non-essentials in a modern-judicial framework. Acclaimed Professor of Law Faizan Mustafa has pointed out in his Hindustan Times article the reductive approach to see Islam in terms of essentiality and non-essentiality by the court:" in the Shirur Mutt case in 1954. The court held that the term "religion" would cover all rituals and practices "integral" to a religion, and took upon itself the responsibility of determining the essential and non-essential practices of a religion. The essentiality/integrality doctrine has tended to lead the court into an area beyond its competence and given judges the power to decide purely religious questions." He goes on to say that there is no particular system to define the essential and non-essentials of religion. He says," — in some cases, it (the court) has relied on religious texts to determine essentiality, in others on the empirical behaviour of followers, and in yet others, based on whether the practice existed at the time the religion originated". This ambiguous nature of making assumptions about a community of 200 + million followers just on the premises of behaviour patterns and the origins of practice should be thoroughly countered. In their intellectual history, Muslim scholars have had many differences in various respects; they still have differences in various practises and behaviours. Still, there has been a common consensus as well on multiple issues.

Suppose the court appoints Islamic scholarly groups who are rightly versed in Islamic jurisprudence to decide on any religious practices of Muslims. In that case, it will be an altogether different scenario, but such is not the case. The subjective biases of the judiciary and the default Hindu social system treat the Muslim community according to their ethics and the terms of a system that is indifferent to Islamic sensibilities.

Having established that the argument of the non-essentiality of the hijab is theologically unfounded and erroneous, we should nevertheless remember that minority religious rights cannot be conditional upon essentiality. Hijab is essential, but we resist the ban not merely based on how integral to faith it is but because we have a right to observe all aspects of our faith, even optional ones. A defence based on the essentiality of a practice threatens several other aspects of our lives, which may not be Islamically compulsory but form a part of our lives, such as beef consumption. Cow vigilantes have been regularly killing Muslims because of beef consumption or dealing in cow products. Beef is not an essential part of a Muslim's diet, but our consumption must not be hindered based on this argument. A problematic outcome of the view of essentiality was seen in 1994 when the Supreme Court of India passed a judgement that said, "A mosque is not an essential part of the practice of the religion of Islam and namaz (prayer) by Muslims can be offered anywhere, even in the open". This verdict was later used in 2010 by Allahabad High court to hand over several acres of land around the disputed Babri Masjid to the government because Muslims should not claim anything the court deems non-essential.

Legislation, Muslim Law and Practices

Beyond the immediate communalisation and polarisation, it is expected that the sudden mobilisation around the hijab is a precursor to the BJP's agenda of the Uniform Civil Code(UCC). The UCC proposes the imposition of a uniform law in a country of 1.3 billion people with multiple religions and customs. Currently, minorities, including Muslims, have the freedom to follow their personal law in matters such as marriage and inheritance. The UCC has been an agenda of the BJP for a long time and seeks to impose a majoritarian law on all communities. The attack on the hijab is expected to skyrocket into a demand for scrapping all displays of faith in public life and form the agenda for the next elections in 2024.

The attack on the hijab was not exactly unexpected. The BJP government has been actively interfering with Muslim personal laws and private life since the inception of its term in 2014. In its first term, it raised the issue of Triple Talaq, and in its second term, it passed the Triple Talaq bill to prove its saviourship of Muslim women. From then onwards, BJP has tried to show itself as a saviour and protector of Muslim women from "oppression". It should be naturally assumed that the "oppressor" in this context could be none other than Muslim men and Islamic practices and principles enshrined in any Muslim society. The BJP has also recently dedicated May 1 as Muslim Women's Day to celebrate the passing of the Triple Talaq Bill in 2019. Such events are necessary to whitewash the BJP's violence committed against Muslim women. The question is not ultimately of practices but the insertion of majoritarian dominated ideologies to alter the Muslim practices to "civilise" Muslims according to the majority's will. All infringements on the rights of Muslims are presented as gifts to Muslim women. Post the eruption of controversy against the hijab, Narendra Modi spoke at a rally claiming to fight the elements(implied Muslim men) who are keeping Muslim betiyan (daughters) away from education.

It is a commonly held perception that Indian Muslims restrict their daughters from receiving education due to entrenched patriarchal notions in Islamic ideology and upbringing, which is responsible for low literacy levels among Muslim women. However, according to the most important survey and report on Indian Muslims conducted by the Sachar committee in 2006, such arguments were found to be baseless. The report outlined the ghettoisation of Muslims, the lack of good schools in specifically Muslim areas, discrimination in classrooms against Muslim students, and girls' safety as the main reason for low literacy rates among them.

All the efforts in "securing" Muslim women's rights should be seen as rhetoric to "protect" Muslim women from "intra-community" oppression, but in reality, the purpose is nothing but to infringe and modify the Islamic or cultural practices of Muslims. Overall, the more de-islamised a Muslim becomes, the more acceptable they become to the majoritarian system and can better practice a form of nationalism that is itself heavily religious.

The tricky relation between feminity, nationalism and Indian Muslims lies firstly in the personification of nations as a woman, which is a common feature of countries around the globe and not just in India. Since Muslims are symbolised as invaders, foreigners, and looters, they are also cast as rapists, fraud Romeos waging "Love jihad" to honeytrap and impregnate Hindu women. This image is conveniently conflated with the image of India as a feminine figure whose dignity is not respected by invaders or those who are not the "sons of the land". This personification is compounded by the deification of Bharat Mata (Mother India) as a female Hindu Goddess. Now not only do Muslims refuse to personify the land, but the deification also goes against the very essence of La ilaaha Illalah. This rhetoric has been weaponised to such an extent that often, Muslims are lynched to death for refusing to chant "Bharat Mata ki Jai" (Glory to Mother India).

The Role of Global Muslims

There is little to be done as long as the matter is subjudice. However, demonstrations of solidarity go a long way. We saw international protests in several countries in support of the Muslim girls. To bring the issue of brimming apartheid against Indian Muslims before global media will hopefully make the Indian courts consider the external perspective. It is necessary to amplify the voices of

Indian Muslim women and keep a keen eye on political developments in India. Indian Muslims are aware of global Muslims' support of our cause. We recognise that the government of several Muslim countries do not represent the masses. These governments' lack of official statements does not represent the ummah solidarity between ordinary Muslims. Finally, nothing can beat the power of dua'a. If one is not capable of demonstrations, media campaigns and political pressure, they must remember dua'a overpowers every other force.

Concluding thoughts

This toxic role of saviourship and guardianship by Hindu fascists of Muslim women leads to such assumption that each minority Muslim party is by nature "fundamentalist" and works to "brainwash" Muslim women to protest for something dogmatic like Hijab/Niqab, which Muslim women essentially do not require. This is the same saviour trope of "mission civilisatrice" practised by colonial France over its colonies. The agenda is the annexation of Muslim women's autonomy by criminalising the immediate societal structures in which Muslim women are born and brought like the Muslim male, the Muslim family, the religious institutions, the practices, cultures, traditions, histories, etc. They attempt to isolate Muslim women from all things Muslim and pose as the sole guardians and arbitrators of their lives and bodies.

Finally, the question for us should be, what are the limitations of state institutions to meddling with minority practices? Should there be religious scholarly bodies to aid courts regarding the issue of the practice of religion? Can the secular court and state have the authority to legislate on the practices of minorities? And most importantly, where and when does the infringement stop? What is the assurance of no further encroachment on the faith of Indian Muslims? When writing this piece, the Karnataka High Court has passed its final verdict on the issue and has banned the hijab in all institutes that prescribe a uniform.

Writers: Hanan Khaja is an engineer and independent writer from India. Mohd Kashif is a Muslim student activist and postgraduate from JNU. Editor: Farhat Amin

ABOUT THE AUTHOR

Farhat Amin is an author & host of the podcast, her books include Smart Teenage Muslimah, Smart Single Muslimah and Child Loss, Bereavement & Hope. She has delivered lectures & courses on Women in Islam and feminism. She shares life advice that is Islamic and honest thought-provoking via her website www.smartmuslima.com. Her aim is to help women achieve confidence in their faith. The inspiration for both her website and podcast is Surah Asr:

"By Time. The human being is in loss. Except those who believe, and do good works, and encourage truth, and recommend patience."

She felt there was a need for a platform that represents Muslim women without falling into the temptation of watering down Islam for the sake of mass appeal. As Islam encourages hikmah (wisdom) when informing others of Islam, not compromise.

REFERENCES

[1] https://www.cage.ngo/wp-content/uploads/2021/01/HRC-Complaint-Procedure-Form-SLS.pdf
[22] https://www.cage.ngo/global-coalition-demands-un-human-rights-council-take-legal-action-against-france-for-abuse-of-muslims
[3] ibid
[4] Lila Abu-Lughod, Do Muslim Women Need Saving?
[5] https://www.sacredfootsteps.org/2021/03/21/unveiling-the-algerienne-french-colonial-photography/
[6] Frantz Fanon, Algeria Unveiled, Decolonisation: Perspectives From Now And Then
[7] https://www.theguardian.com/world/2002/sep/21/gender.usa?CMP=share_btn_tw
[8] https://watson.brown.edu/costsofwar/costs/human/civilians/afghan
[9] L. Ahmed, Women and Gender in Islam
[10] https://traversingtradition.com/2020/06/05/hijab-not-my-body-not-my-choice/
www.huffpost.com/entry/progressive-muslims-launch-gay-friendly-women-led-mosques
[12] www.thedailybeast.com/airport-security-lets-profile-muslims.
[13] https://www.theguardian.com/theobserver/2010/mar/21/debate-on-french-burka-ban
[14] www.bidoun.org/issues/28-interviews
[15] A,Wadud, Inside the Gender Jihad, p,220
[16] https://www.independent.co.uk/voices/taliban-sharia-law-muslim-feminist-women-b1905249.html
[17] https://www.bidoun.org/issues/28-interviews
[18] Khan, Mariam. It's Not about the Burqa. Picador, 2019
[19] Eltahawy, Mona. Headscarves and Hymens: Why the Middle East Needs a Sexual Revolution. Farrar, Straus and Giroux, 2016
[20] https://www.britannica.com/event/womens-movement
[21] https://www.theguardian.com/commentisfree/2012/oct/12/anti-muslim-hate-speech-mona-eltahawy
[22] https://www.pri.org/stories/2012-10-22/four-questions-mona-eltahawy
[23] https://en.wikipedia.org/wiki/Muhammad_bin_Saud
[24] Nicolas Sarkozy. *Is France Right to Ban the Burka in Public? | The Debate ...* www.theguardian.com/theobserver/2010/mar/21/debate-on-french-burka-ban.

[25] 25 https://www.prnewswire.co.uk/news-releases/islamic-clothing-market-size-worth-88-35-billion-by-2025-cagr-5-0-grand-view-research-inc--820570235.html
[26] https://eu.usatoday.com/story/life/fashion/2020/11/26/halima-aden-model-who-wears-hijab-takes-step-back-fashion/6432684002/
[27] https://qarawiyyinproject.co/2017/11/25/people-think-hijab-sexualises-young-girls-because-of-the-muslim-community/
[28] https://en.wikipedia.org/wiki/The_Beauty_Myth
[29] 29 https://eu.usatoday.com/story/life/fashion/2020/11/26/halima-aden-model-who-wears-hijab-takes-step-back-fashion/6432684002/
[30] https://www.theguardian.com/uk-news/2019/sep/15/lifestyle-website-for-muslim-teens-is-covertly-funded-by-the-home-office
[31] https://www.theguardian.com/uk-news/2019/sep/15/lifestyle-website-for-muslim-teens-is-covertly-funded-by-the-home-office

Printed in Dunstable, United Kingdom